When Kathy is Keith

Wallace Wong, R. Psy.

To order additional copies of this book, contact:
Xlibris Corporation
1-888-795-4274
www.Xlibris.com
Orders@Xlibris.com

DEDICATION

From Kathy to Keith was inspired by many transgender children and youth that I have worked with. I am often amazed by their spirits, strengths, and courage. Their stories have touched my heart in so many ways. I hope parents, teachers, and other professionals will read this book with an open mind and try to see it from the view points of a transgender child or youth. It is then that you will truly understand what a transgender child or youth is really going through. To all my transgender clients, thank you for being yourselves. To Steven, thank you for being my support. Don't know how I could do it without you.

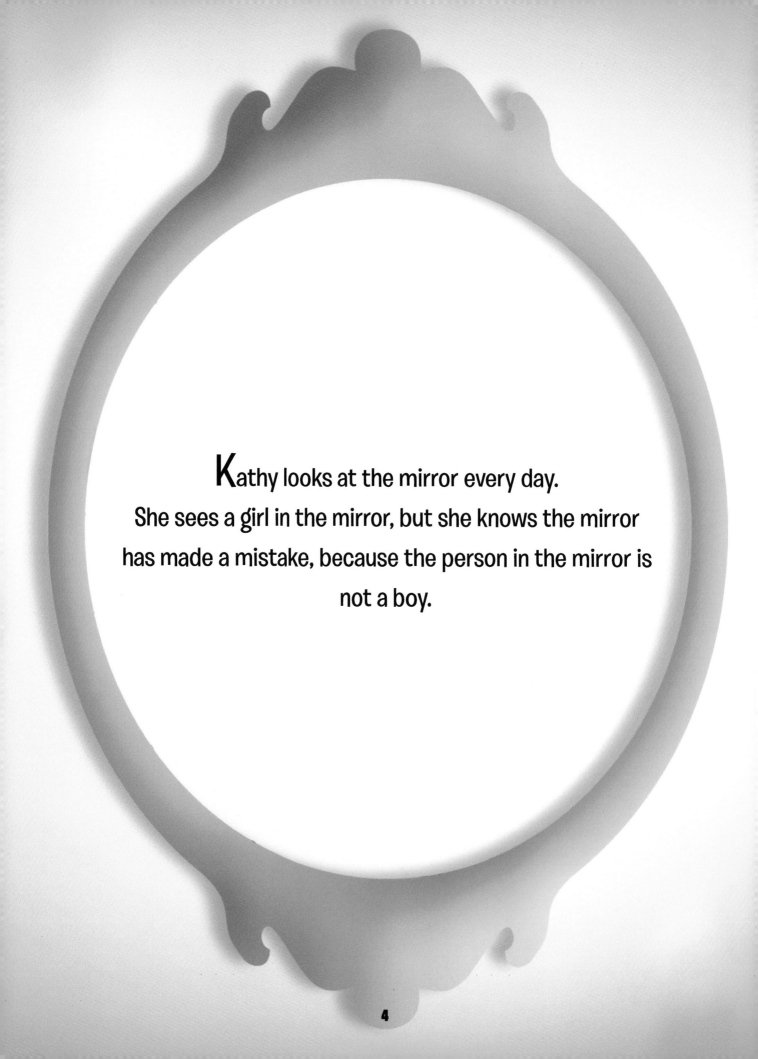

Kathy looks at the mirror every day.
She sees a girl in the mirror, but she knows the mirror
has made a mistake, because the person in the mirror is
not a boy.

She tells her friends that she is a boy, not a girl. Her friends make fun of her because of this.

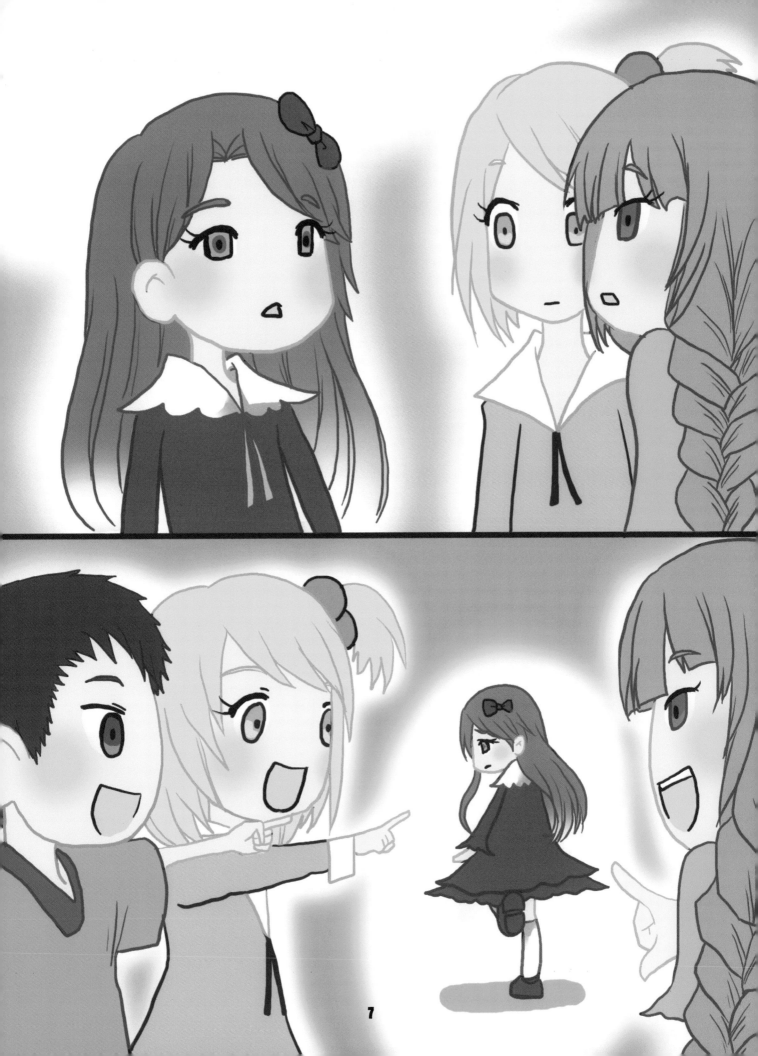

She tells her teacher that she is a boy, not a girl.
Her teacher tells Kathy is being silly.

She tells her parents that she is a boy, not a girl.
They tell Kathy that she will grow out of it.

Kathy feels very lonely because no one seems to understand her. No one believes that she is a boy, not a girl.

Christmas is coming in two weeks.
Kathy's mother is taking Kathy to the mall to take
pictures with Santa Claus.

Kathy is excited, because she wants to tell Santa what she really wants for Christmas.
The line is long, but Kathy does not mind waiting!

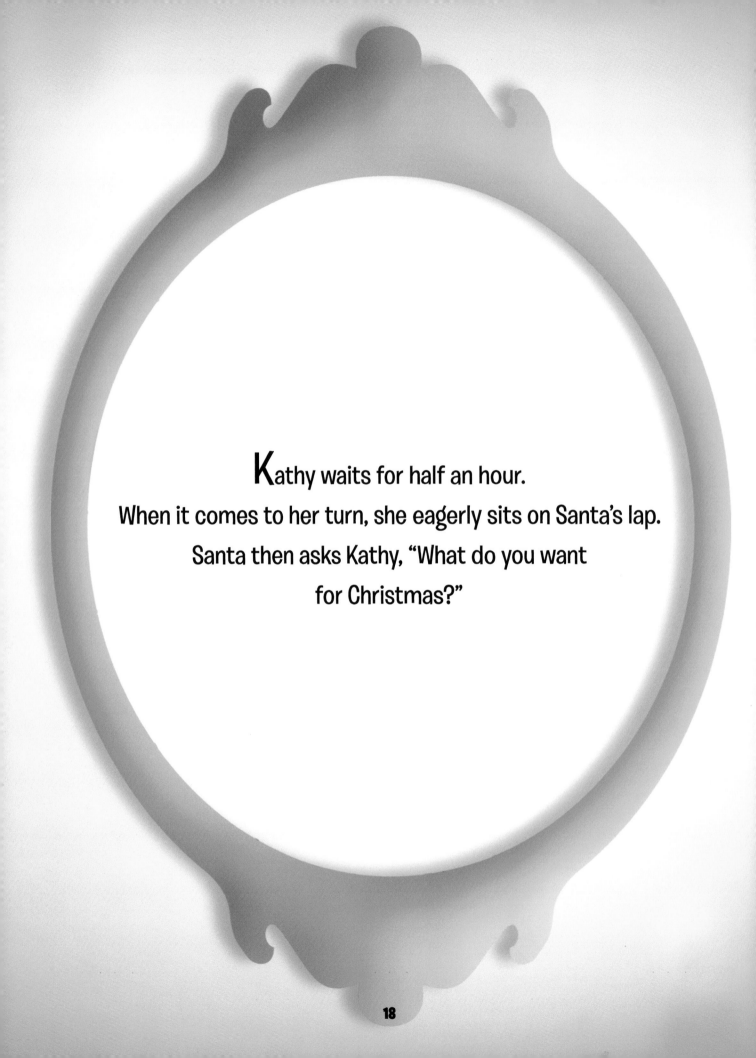

Kathy waits for half an hour.
When it comes to her turn, she eagerly sits on Santa's lap.
Santa then asks Kathy, "What do you want
for Christmas?"

Kathy looks at Santa's eyes and says, "I want to be a boy. Santa, can you please make me into a boy!" Santa is surprised by Kathy's request, and does not know what to say to her.

Kathy's mother feels embarrassed but also feels that Kathy really meant it when she asked Santa that question.

When they get home, Kathy's mother asks Kathy, "Do you really see yourself as a boy?"
Kathy nods without any hesitation.

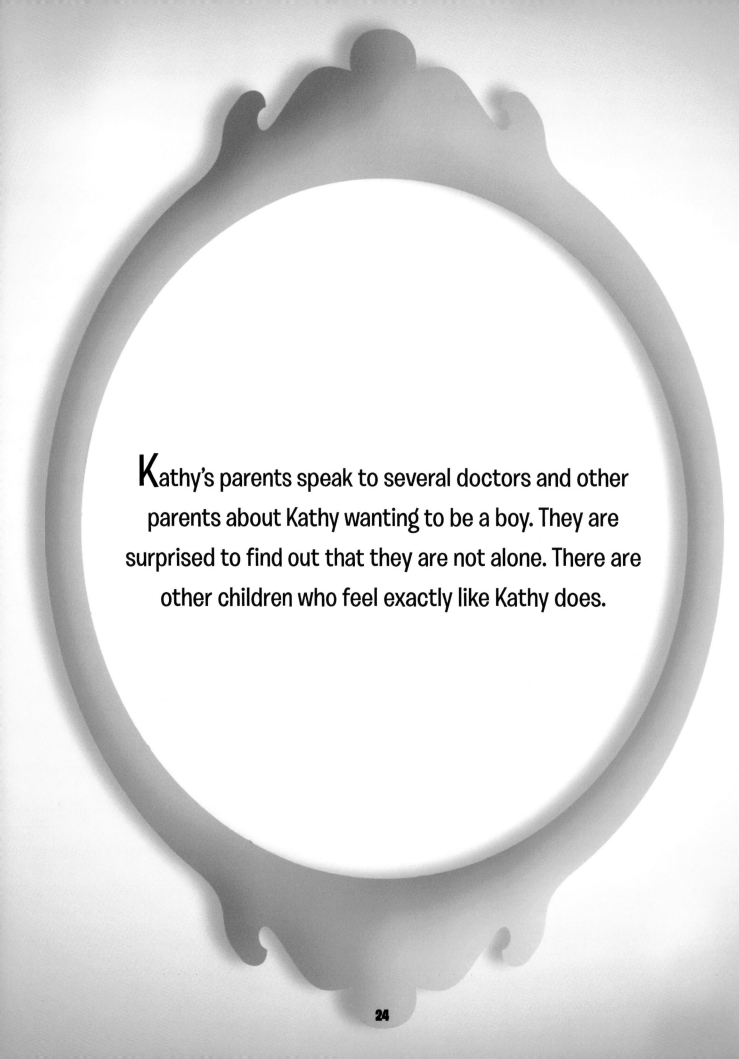

Kathy's parents speak to several doctors and other parents about Kathy wanting to be a boy. They are surprised to find out that they are not alone. There are other children who feel exactly like Kathy does.

School Principal

Kathy's parents decide to let Kathy gradually live her life as a boy.
They first let Kathy change her name to "Keith".

They also let Keith wear boy's clothes at home. They notice Keith has become happier and less sad since he has been allowed to be a boy.

Keith knows that not everyone will understand what he is going through, but that his parents will always be there for him.

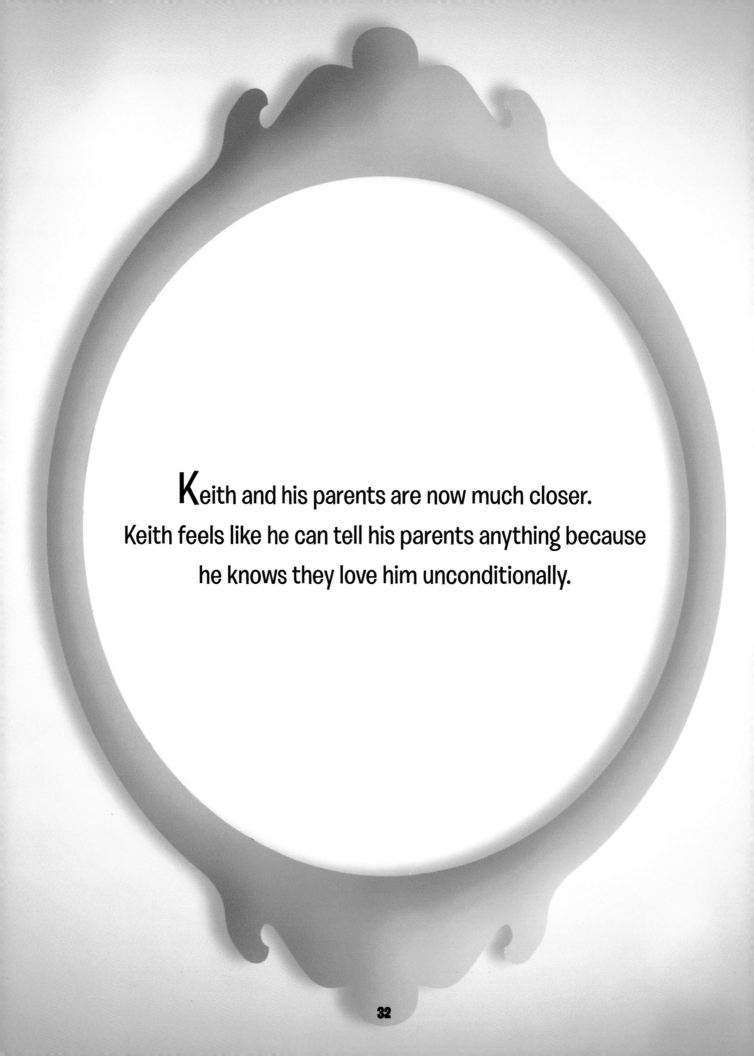

Keith and his parents are now much closer.
Keith feels like he can tell his parents anything because
he knows they love him unconditionally.

The End

Support/Information:

www.pflagvancouver.com

http://www.apa.org/topics/sexuality/transgender.aspx#

http://transhealth.vch.ca/

http://www.trans-academics.org/about_us

CPSIA information can be obtained
at www.ICGtesting.com
Printed in the USA
LVIC06n1122280914
406232LV00015B/87

* 9 7 8 1 4 6 5 3 7 1 4 1 6 *